How To Get Married . . .
and Stay Married

How To Get Married...
and Stay Married

DR. WILLIE TAPLIN BARROW

Cool Springs Publishing, Inc.
Colorado Springs, CO
Chicago, IL

HOW TO GET MARRIED ... AND STAY MARRIED
Copyright © 2004 by Willie Taplin Barrow

For more information please write:
Cool Springs Publishing House
3710 River Road
Hazel Crest, IL 60429

Barrow, Willie Taplin, 1924 –
How To Get Married ... and Stay Married

Editing by Steve Wamberg and Innovative Computer Resources, LLC, Chicago, IL, Cover Design by Innovative Computer Resources, LLC, Chicago, IL

Printed in the United States of America

ISBN   1-889860-07-7

FOREWORD

It is a profound honor and delight to have been asked to pen these words about my dearest friend, colleague and sister in the faith, the Reverend Mrs. Willie Taplan Barrow, as she reflects upon marriage and its many challenges today.

"Willie B," as she is affectionately known by family and friends, or the "little warrior," which has become her designation to a generation of social and political activists, has been and continues to be a mentor and mother to many.

I met Willie and her husband Clyde, called "Honey" by those who really knew him, nearly forty years ago. Their marriage was a unique partnership. In numerous ways they were polar opposites. Honey was shy, reticent, retiring, and shunned the spotlight, while Willie is gregarious, direct, dynamic, and for close to fifty years, a leading advocate and public presence in the struggle for racial justice. Honey was a homebody, and took care of all the responsibilities related to their home and private world.

What a blessed arrangement for Willie, who has never been still, but always on the go in this nation and around the globe! Both had a unique appreciation for the other, and allowed each other the space to be who they were as individuals.

They shared a son Keith who they loved, in the words of Edgar Allen Poe, "with a love that was more than love." Keith was a miracle child conceived after many barren years through Willie's prayers, fasting, and the power of God to do great and amazing things.

Willie Taplin Barrow has much to say about life, living, struggling, grieving, hoping, and being. She has brought all these things together in this short and pithy book about getting and staying married. Read it, be enlightened, encouraged and most of all, blessed.

Rev. Calvin S. Morris, Ph.D.
Executive Director
Community Renewal Society
Chicago, Illinois

INTRODUCTION

Not long ago, a woman I know asked me for a letter of recommendation to move into a prestigious building. Problem was, she was shacking up with a man at the time, and had been for eight years.

I told her when that man married her, I'd give her the letter. She called me back the next day and told me the man said he'd pack his bags and leave her first.

What do we have against marriage? Do we feel like marriages are a lost cause because over half of them fall apart in this country? Do we think we're so advanced that we can manage society without a declaration of partnership between man and woman before God and those around us?

If so, it's time to get the water out of our heads! It's time to value marriage as the divine partnership it is. We've been mixed up too long about this.

The U.S. Census Bureau tells us that nearly half the marriages entered into today will likely end in divorce. That's a prediction. What we do know from recent history is that marriages that started later in the 20th century didn't last as long as those from the earlier part of the century. The report made it clear that divorce throws a number of women into poverty.[1] As of the year 2000, an estimated one million children were involved annually in families of divorce.[2]

Several years ago, my husband Clyde and I repeated our vows to each other after more than half a century of marriage. It was a very special day. When I repeated my vows, I called up ABC, NBC, CNN, and the *Chicago Tribune*. I said to each reporter, "I am getting ready to repeat my vows after 52 years of marriage to the same man. You all cover all the negative stuff about Black people. Now I want you to cover one of the most positive things about Black people. I am walking down the aisle at the Vernon Park Church of God, and my husband and I are walking

---

[1]Kreider, Rose M. and Jason M. Fields, 2001. *Number, Timing, and Duration of Marriages and Divorces: Fall 1996.* Current Population Reports, P70-80. U.S. Census Bureau, Washington, DC.
[2]http://www.divorcemag.com/statistics/statsUS.shtml. Accessed 5/30/2004.

down that aisle with *100 other couples* who have been married 25 years or more. The oldest couple's been married 77 years!" (They walked down that aisle, with me right there.)

I said, "I want you to come and bring your spouses because you all need to see for yourself." And every camera showed up, and those reporters even invited their spouses to come with them.

When they interviewed me after that ceremony, here's what I told them: "I'm planning my funeral right now and I want you all to do a video presentation of my life. And this needs to be one big section in it: 'How to get married and stay married.' That's that."

Marriage must be restored to its place as part of the divine order. When we engage in relationships that have no definition, we invite chaos. Chaos in our families brings chaos in our world.

God's children deserve better. You need to know why marriage is a blessing, not a burden. You need to understand how to get married, and stay married. That's why I wrote this book.

> The Rev. Willie Talpin Barrow
> Chicago, Illinois
> June 2004

WHOLE MARRIAGE FOR WHOLE PEOPLE

God made marriage a unique kind of partnership in His creation.

God created everything in this world. He first made everything in this world for man to survive. He made enough fowl in the air, fish of the sea, and beasts of the field. He made the ocean, the sky, and the moon. He created everything. How He did it, I'm not too sure. But He took enough time to create a world; and that world was for man's survival. After God did that, he sat down and he rested (something we don't have the sense enough to do)!

Then God gave it some thought: "Who is going to run my world? Who is really going to run my world? I need some managers to manage my creation."

Then He said, "Let me see," and He scooped up some sand, some dirt; and breathed into that dirt His Spirit. And man became a what? *A living soul.*

Man became a living soul. God already had His angels. He already had the beasts of the field and the fowl of the air; the moon, the stars. He already had all that. He scooped down and breathed into that dirt His spirit and man became a living soul; wherefore He called that soul "Adam."

Now, before He would release Adam into creation, God said, "Adam, I already have angels, and these wild animals, but I'm going to make you a little lower than the angels and a little higher than the beasts." What makes us a little lower than the angels and a little higher than the beasts is called *intellect* or *intelligence*. So man is different from a monkey, or a bear, or a cow. He is somewhat "elevated"—he is God's image-bearer to represent Him. However, even in man's elevated position in creation, God had more to give him. He said, "I am going to make you a helpmeet. I've got to give you a partner."

What is a helpmeet? A partner, a balance, once you realize God's purpose and intention for your being as a manager of His creation. It is someone who is comparable to, and who complements you.

God didn't name anything. He made the *nature* of His creation, and after He made Adam, He told him to do the naming. That was man's first task as manager of His creation. The beasts of the field and the fowl of the air; every bird, we named them; every animal, man named them. Why? *Because God gave us the intellect to do it.* And when Adam was done naming the animals, having looked at all of them he could, there was none comparable to him. There was no helpmeet to be found among the animals.

So God made a helpmeet comparable to Adam. Let's set the record straight. The function of the female was first set forth as being an *intellectual* balance to the male, not just a sexual balance. God indeed told Eve and Adam that she would bear children. But first, He made it clear to them that *they were intelligent beings.* Women are not sex objects to be manipulated; they are subjects to be understood. It was *after* God made the intellectual helpmeet-partner balance that He told Adam and Eve, "There's got to be more than just you two here. I want you to replenish the earth and bear children." That's just one part of our creation.

Another part of creation is our *responsibility to the next generation.* The reason why God told the woman to replenish the earth is because she's the one who gets pregnant and carries that baby for nine months before anyone else has access to it. Nobody has access to the unborn but a woman. So she has to be careful how she thinks, what she says, what she eats, what her attitudes are; because all those things affect the baby in her womb. All those things become part of that child before he or she even sees the earth.

Likewise, it is the same with the daddy of that child. Every part of his life will somehow affect the child. Men have to be very aware that although women are the carriers of life and nursery of life, both partners have a God-ordained responsibility to the child that is part of His creation design. Therefore, the partners have to be very mindful of that.

The child is also affected by generations gone before even if he or she has never seen his grandpa, never seen his granny. What those generations took in attitudinally, what they ate physically, what they consumed mentally and spiritually all affected that child.

So let's get back to marriage. What is it, anyway? It is a God-ordained partnership between a woman and a man. This means equal in God's sight, where "equal" doesn't necessarily mean "the same." It is honorable in God's creation. It is pleasurable and purposeful. It recognizes each partner as a person created in God's image.

There's a commercial out now: "If a woman says she'll call you, she'll call you this evening; if a man says he'll call you, he'll call you before he dies—or he may not call at all." That's just one difference between a man and a woman. Here's another: A woman, the way God made her, can do one, two, three, four, five, six things at one time; whereas a man can hardly do two at one time and keep his sanity. (If that's you, laugh and say, "Amen!" If not, just pray for me!)

God says we need each other, and not just for procreation. God ordained marriage between man and wife; women and men. He didn't ask nobody about whether or not marriage was a good idea. He didn't go on a research hunt. He didn't conduct any focus groups. He just scooped His intentions right out of the dust of the earth and breathed life into them so we can be in partnership with each other. The way we are created, men and women are automatically partners by design.

We must understand God's intention in this partnership. We must consider marriage as one means of managing God's creation. We must know that marriage is one way God will complement and complete many of us for whom "it is not good to be alone."

There are three aspects of marriage that you need to consider before even discussing the subject with another person: the spiritual, the practical and the physical. These issues are crucial before you marry, and just as important to discuss regularly after you take your vows.

Marriage will affect every area of your life. You need to take a look at the whole picture to have a whole marriage—and be whole people in that marriage.

One

THE SPIRITUAL ASPECT OF MARRIAGE

I believe that most people are missing out on the number one principle for a successful marriage: *It takes three to be married: man, woman, and God.*

Take a walk with me. When I first met Clyde Raymond Barrow in 1942, he was not a churchgoing man. I was a student at Warner Pacific Theological Seminary in Portland, Oregon when we met. One day, I was getting off the bus and walking up the hill to the college campus. This guy got out and followed me. He called out, "Baby!"

I kept walking, and he said, "Didn't you hear me speak to you?"

I looked around and I said, "You weren't speaking to me, were you? Because you don't know me. Why were you calling me 'Baby'?"

He said, "If you don't answer back, I'll whip your little butt."

I said, "You *certainly* don't know who you're talking to." And I kept walking, just kept walking.

Meanwhile, I didn't have money to pay my tuition so I was looking for a job. It was during World War II. Somebody told me to go to Kaiser Shipyard; they were training new workers because most of the men were going away to the service.

I went to Kaiser Shipyard and went through the training.

I trained at Kaiser Shipyard at night and became a welder. Then about three months later, I was welding one day and this guy came up to me and said, "What you doing out here?"

I said, "Who are you?"

He answered, "Don't tell me you don't know me. I met you when you were getting off the bus. Remember? You cursed me out."

And I said, "I don't curse."

He wasn't done. He said, "I told you I was going to whip your little butt."

And I said, "Oh, *you're* the guy?"

He said yes, he was. We were working at the same place. So I invited him to come to church. He said, "Sure, I'll come."

Clyde came to church the following Sunday, and he kept going to church after that. He used to come to church mostly to see me, but he did start going—and that's how we started our relationship.

To tell the truth, it wasn't like we were always at the same place at the same time spiritually. But we did know, together, that God had to be a part of our relationship if we were to be married.

After 56 years of marriage to the same man, I believe more than ever that God must be at the core of a solid marriage. So here are the questions I ask couples who are looking at the spiritual aspect of marriage together.

1. How long have you known each other?

You need to find out about a person's background spiritually. You need to know someone long enough to know that they aren't putting on a show by going to church. You also need to know about a person's family, and the models for marriage and partnership he or she grew up with.

2. How did you meet?

I don't ask that couples meet at a local church, because Clyde and I didn't meet that way. And I don't think "meeting" someone is always the same as the first time you see that person. But your relationship should be based on some kind of meeting as equals. (And remember, "equal" doesn't necessarily mean "the same.")

3. What attracted you to your partner?

Sometimes we just meet people and say, "She's good looking," or "He's got a good job." Then we say, "I want to marry that person!" That's not the way you choose a partner. You need to sit down and talk and get to know about the other person's character. You need to learn how to appreciate who

God has created that person to be. If there's nothing there that attracts you, you need to find someone else.

4. Were you reared in a Christian home?

The home you grew up in will affect your marriage spiritually. If you saw a model of a spiritually healthy marriage growing up, you have a better idea of how to attain a spiritually healthy marriage yourself.

5. What is your church background?

If you and your partner-to-be have different church backgrounds, have you considered belonging to the same church? Can you settle that issue before you are married, so you can be more unified as a married couple? Even though I am in the civil rights movement, I was in the reformation movement long before the civil rights movement because my mother was Methodist and my daddy was Baptist. They had to reform their beliefs. My mother came over into the Baptist community because my daddy convinced her that "sprinkling" wasn't gonna get her delivered. Only baptism. So she finally came over. They adjusted.

6. Have both of you made a personal commitment to Jesus Christ as your Savior and Lord?

The Bible says that believers and unbelievers should avoid entering into marriage together. I believe that this is as much for the sake of the unbeliever as the believer in a marriage. It's just too frustrating not to have common ground here.

7. Do you understand Christian marriage to be submission to each other?

The Bible clearly says in Ephesians that Christians in marriage should "...submit yourselves one to another." The whole passage talks about how a wife should give herself to her husband, and how the husband should lay down his life for his wife. But, most of the time, we use that scripture so the husband can say to his wife, "Submit yourself to me because I am the man." That's not what that scripture means—"I am the man." No, it simply means, "Be partners in Jesus Christ."

8. Is there any impediment to this marriage?

All your issues need to be out on the table before you enter into marriage. Don't assume anything. Take the time to talk through your doubts, your hopes, and your dreams together. If anything comes up that makes either partner say, "Whoa!" you need to wait to get married.

9. What place does the Lord's Church play in your life now? How about the future?

You need someplace to build community. The church provides that kind of place.

The day may come when you need help for your marriage or your family. The church can provide spiritual support when you hurt. The church can provide practical support for you in those times of need.

10. What are you doing, and what will you do, to encourage mutual growth in the Lord?

You should be spiritually healthy as you enter into marriage. You need to do what you can to encourage your partner's spiritual growth, too. Give her the time for personal devotions. Buy him a Bible he enjoys reading. When both partners in a marriage are growing toward God, they will likely not grow apart.

11. Do you pray together now? If not, will you begin to share in this spiritual experience?

I've never been able to say to a couple, "You pray too much! Stop it!" We've all heard the old saying, "The family that prays together, stays together." I'm going to bring it even closer to what we've been discussing here and say, "The couple that prays together, stays together!" Couples need to spend more time learning how to pray together *before* their wedding day.

12. Will you plan a wedding ceremony that will exalt the Lord Jesus Christ?

You already know that I believe it takes three to be married: man, woman, and God. I would encourage you to consider how you will bring God into your wedding ceremony in a way that lets everyone know He is the heart of your marriage.

I kept God at the head of my marriage for 56 years. Clyde and I had our share of trials, as you will find out. But the one thing that kept us together all that time was the spiritual side of our marriage. When everything else was falling apart, when I was ready to give up, God was our Sure Source.

Notes

_____

_____

_____

_____

_____

_____

_____

Notes

_____

_____

_____

_____

_____

_____

_____

THE PRACTICAL ASPECT OF MARRIAGE

There are many practical issues to consider in marriage, but one comes to mind more than the others: money. Money is probably the biggest practical problem in marriage.

Money, money, money. This is one thing I have a healthy background in, because my parents were united when it came to money. I never heard my daddy say, "Mine." I never heard my mother say, "Mine." It was "our house, our car, our money." But when it's "my money, my check," it's not going nowhere. It's just not going to work. In singleness, if you have three cars, they're "your cars." But, in a marriage, they become "our cars."

It's a real situation figuring out who should handle the budget. So, who should manage the budget? It's whoever can handle it best. And don't forget to put yourselves in that budget. If you have a budget for your car note and your house note, then you should also put a personal allowance in your budget. Don't just use a credit card for special treats, get in debt over your head and be suffering from a deficit. Put your allowance in your personal budget.

You may be saying, "I work every day. Even if I stay home, I still work every day. Being stuck here with the children, stuck cleaning the house is a hard job. I deserve an allowance. I deserve $50 a day, or maybe per week." Whatever your budget says, put in allowances for yourselves. Be sure you put those in, even if your allowance is $10 a week.

I am a tither in my church. I tithe and I convinced my husband to make that a household practice. But his allowance was his to do with as he pleased. For many years, our allowances—after we paid for the gas in the car, stocked up on food for the week, and everything else—were $10 a week each.

My husband had money because he used his allowance well. My husband never did a lot of shopping, so he kept his ten dollars. Some of the guys who worked with him couldn't make their money stretch until the next payday. So my husband loaned them money that they could pay back, with interest, at the next payday. The money he loaned them didn't come out of our budget, it came out of <u>his allowance</u>. Sometimes Clyde had $100 or $200 in his pocket because he made his $10 a week work so well. He had money practically all the time but it came out of his allowance because he didn't spend it all every week. Balance again—Clyde was not a spender, he was a saver and investor.

We all had an allowance. I had my $10 allowance, he had his. And then when our son Keith was growing up, we gave him an allowance. So all three of us dealt with our allowances. When Keith grew up, before he went to college, he kept a budget. When he went to college and finished, he got his masters degree on his own and his Ph.D. on his own because he learned about money when he was a little child. If he overspent his allowance budget for popcorn or ice cream or whatever, that was it for the week. That was his allowance. Mama and Daddy had allowances. So did he.

We have really been that kind of family with money. I just keep a book that tells me where the money goes. Most of us don't even know how much we spend. How much money do you spend in a week? If you want practical success in your marriage, you don't just go shopping. You go shopping based on your budget. Money, money, money. Money causes too many problems in our families. Many times we spend all this money we don't have. As a result, money is just killing our marriages and our families.

So, marriage means a series of practical adjustments. Marriage is hard work. It's a job, and don't you fool yourself by thinking it's not. People who don't want to work often get divorced, because you have to work at marriage.

That's why it's important to answer some practical questions when you're thinking about marriage. Here are some that many couples tell me have been important for them to discuss:

1. **What are your future spouse's strongest and weakest points?**

God gives us partners because we need each other. When you know each other's strengths and weaknesses, you know where you need to help fill in a gap for your partner. You know where you need your partner to help you, too.

2. Do you get along with your prospective in-laws?

Some people don't want to believe this, but when you marry your spouse, you really do marry your spouse's family, too. Their concerns become your concerns, because you share your life with your spouse. If you can't stand your future spouse's family, you need to think about whether that person is who you want to share your life with. (And, an attitude adjustment might not hurt, either!)

3. Do you know what your total income will be?

You need a realistic idea of how much money you'll be needing and making. Some couples think they can live off of next to nothing, and so how much money they'll make doesn't matter to them. Other couples think they need a small fortune to get married, and that's not realistic, either. No matter what your viewpoint is, money matters.

4. Have you planned a tentative budget?

You can save yourself your first three arguments if you put a budget together before you get married!

5. Who will be "president," and who will be "secretary-treasurer" in your home?

This is a practical question. It isn't about position, it's about function. Once again, it's about managing God's creation. Some partners need to make executive-type decisions for the home, ranging from which groceries to buy to which stocks to watch. Others need to see to it that everyday things are covered, like paying bills and carpooling and writing letters to family. It isn't that partners need to be locked in positions. It's that you need to assign tasks according to each partner's skills and limitations.

6. Do you have the same interests?

You don't need to share every interest, but you do need to have a few interests in common. For example, my husband loved to take vacations. We went to his home country of Belize and Hawaii every now and then. He liked that; he loved to travel, and I do too. That was one thing we did together. Now on Sundays, we'd cook a full "Sunday dinner." I love to cook, and he loved beans and rice and plantains, one of the native dishes in Belize. I knew he loved that and we did that together. I walk in the mornings. I exercise, so I walked five miles, (still do, every day, thank you very much!), and he would walk about a mile. Then he would sit and wait on me. That's what we did special every Saturday morning. There were other interests we had individually that we didn't share together, but we had these things we regularly did together.

7. How do you like each other's friends?

Both partners may need to make adjustments regarding one another's friends. Over the years, my husband Clyde worked his job every day, but he still knew a lot of the people

I knew. We went out to dinner at least twice a week with different friends. One of the most important things you can do is give your friends a positive picture of your partner. That makes it easier for them to appreciate your spouse. Clyde was very proud of me. He let all of his friends know exactly what I was doing, and where I was. And I made sure my friends knew that Clyde was the one who kept me up on the news, which was a big contribution to my work.

8. How do you settle disagreements?

You have to learn how to settle conflict to have a successful marriage. One of the ingredients in my recipe for a successful marriage is, "Disagree if you must, but find ways not to be disagreeable." Don't hold things against your partner. If you discuss something and settle it, then turn it loose. Too many people say to their partner, "This is what you did ten years ago," when they've already discussed it. Well, if you've already discussed it, turn it loose. Let it go! It hurts you physically. It hinders you mentally; and certainly spiritually, and every other way. You can't hold envy and strife. It makes you sick. It frustrates your spouse. It's just not necessary.

9. Are either of you over-dependent on your parents?

Every couple needs to think about this. If one of you is too attached to your parents, you'll have problems setting up the new family you're supposed to start with your spouse. If that's the situation, you may need to physically locate away from those parents so you can learn how to be a partner for your spouse. Marriage is your first job and priority.

10. Is there anything in marriage which you fear?

Even in marriage, most fear is caused by the unknown. Some people fear sharing money. Some people fear moving out of their parents' house. Some people fear commitment. Most of those fears can be settled by talking it out, but you have to take the time to talk it out between yourselves or with a counselor.

11. Have you knowledge of any disease, particularly hereditary, which might affect your future?

The new thing now in medical history is to check your parents' background. Did your father have diabetes? Does high cholesterol run in your mother's family? How about tuberculosis? Partners approaching marriage should check this out. For example, if there is medical history of problems in your family, like diabetes, you may be more likely to have it too. So work together as partners to set up some preventative measures that you can take to not develop the illness. Take precautionary measures so if you get the illness, it doesn't debilitate you. You must find out about health issues in both of your families.

12. Do you have any mutual long-range goals?

You don't have to have a long list of goals, but you need to know that you're working together toward something. For us, owning a house was important. Having things together for when we retired was important. Helping our son grow up to take care of himself and succeed in education was a mutual goal we shared every day.

13. Do you have any outstanding debts? What are your feelings about debts?

When you marry, you are taking on your partner's debts. You need to honestly tell each other the debts you're bringing into the marriage. You also need to agree what will be acceptable debt for you once you're married. A mortgage on a house might be fine. A charge for that plasma television on a credit card with 28% interest isn't.

14. Where will you live? In close proximity to in-laws?

Clyde's family was in Belize and my family was in Texas when we married. We settled for a while on the West Coast and then came to Chicago. That distance forced us how to figure out how to be married to each other on our own terms. Some in-laws can give a couple that kind of distance from a block away, but not many. (Revisit #9).

15. How will marriage make you a better person?

There are many ways marriage can make us better people. We learn a greater appreciation for partnership. We recognize our limitations and strengths. We become better people as we carry out God's intentions. To do this, you must operate in life with purpose. Together in marriage, partners are called to run God's world according to His intentions. That means you respect the uniqueness of your spouse. That means you respect each other's intellect because it comes directly from God. Learning a deeper respect for your partner and God's purpose will surely make you a better person.

16. Do you have a sense of humor?

You have to learn how to laugh with your spouse. You can't take yourselves so seriously that you never laugh at yourselves. You need to mix light moments into your marriage. Life itself will deliver plenty of heavy ones your way.

17. Can you discuss your deepest thoughts and concerns with your partner?

Some people call this finding a "soul mate." It's so important to be hanging out (and I like the words "hanging out") with someone who has a vision on life that is so harmonious with mine that I can be his balance and he can be my balance. That's deep sharing. That's exactly what you need to discuss with your partner: vision, harmony, how to balance one another.

18. Do you really listen to each other?

You have to be in tune enough to know how to hush. And when you pick up those feelings that your partner needs you to listen more than speak, let go; hush. The problem is we can't—and don't—hush. We feel defeated if we have to hush. "Oh, he ain't listening to me." "Oh, she ain't listening to me." "You just tuning me out."

That was a real lesson at first for me, just to hush. Even when I felt that I was not being heard, I had to remind myself, "Hush. Wait a while."

19. How do you treat your parents?

You can't be overdependent on your parents. You can't be cruel to them either. They raised you, so they deserve your respect and love. And your partner's parents raised your partner, so they deserve your respect and love, too. What you need to talk about as a couple is how you will show that love and respect to your parents together.

20. Do you know the state and county laws concerning blood tests and marriage licenses? Who will bring the license to church on your wedding day?

You know how many big, husky men nearly fainted in my office when they found out they'd have to give blood to get a marriage license? You really wouldn't believe how many couples can't lay their hands on the wedding license when it's time to sign it at the church. The point here is to cover all your bases thoroughly. Know what's required. Sometimes you need blood tests, sometimes you need to wait a few days after you receive the license. But take it upon yourselves to know these things and take care of them.

Notes

_____

_____

_____

_____

_____

_____

_____

Notes

_____

_____

_____

_____

_____

_____

_____

Three

THE PHYSICAL ASPECT OF MARRIAGE

I hate to see summer come.

When summer comes, the young ladies are naked. They're showing everything. They think that's womanhood; that's sexy. They don't understand the word "sex." They really don't. And yet when they go through all this "experience" they're seeking and setting themselves up for, they get so upset.

Why? Because they're not satisfied. They take off all their clothes and they're not satisfied. They go on the street and have all of these men. And men don't know what it is either; they don't know. They really don't know their purpose for being here. That's the big problem. They don't know why they are here.

I came up in a disciplined background. I was taught very early that God made you for a particular reason. You're going to grow up and get married, but no sex before marriage. Because, number one, it is unbiblical for you to have sex before you're married.

I believed what my mama and daddy told me about the physical side of man-woman relationships. I really believed. The only thing that was off was that I thought that if a guy touched you, you got pregnant. (It was all in my mind.)

This was how they taught it to us: *Don't let boys be feeling all over you, on all parts of your body.* Well, I grew up like that from the time I had my first little boyfriend through the time I was courting and engaged. In junior high school, I had a little boyfriend who was brought up in the same church I was. So he knew what my family's philosophy was about physical relationships and he never even asked to kiss me, much less try.

Then I left Bentham and went to Houston and stayed with my aunt. There was another guy in Houston. He said, "You like me?"

I told him right then, "I don't like boys to touch me. I don't kiss guys but you can be my friend. Can you abide by that?"

"Yes, yes, yes." (I didn't have any problems there.)

Then I went to seminary. That's when I met my husband. I told him the same thing as that guy in Houston. Clyde didn't touch me and he didn't kiss me. We went to the movies, went to church. He'd drop me off and say, "Good night; bye bye, sweetheart!"

He called me "sweetheart" but he never touched me. Then he proposed. I said we could get married, but no sex before marriage. We were engaged three years.

I already believed in God; that God would supply all my needs if I obeyed him. Scripture says sex before marriage is fornication. Scientists say sexual intimacy before marriage harms a person's ability to be intimate in marriage. Scripture says a married person having sex with someone other than their spouse is adultery. Counselors say adultery introduces emotional and physical threats to everyone involved.

Scripture says, "Obedience *is* better than sacrifice." Obedience is better. Just obey God. Not only when your daddy and mama are looking at you, but when you're in the dark and nobody else is looking at you but God. And God's always looking. Just be yourself; don't be some sexual athlete. That way, when you walk down that aisle you can say to your mate, "I am yours and I am yours all by myself and I was never touched. No one else has ever touched me."

I believe in sexual purity. I don't believe in shacking. I don't have to prove one thing outside marriage to make you know that I am a woman, or to make a man feel that he is a man. He is a man because God made him.

I know my purpose. I have always felt that women are not sex objects to be manipulated but subjects to be understood. When a guy tried to hit on me I told him, "You don't want to hit on my behind, you want to hit on my brain. That's what you're attracted to: my brain. I am a bright and intelligent girl."

I tell women all the time that you have to teach this to the man. You have to let him know that the real reason he's attracted to you is *not* because you have big legs and a back. He's really attracted to that intellect God gave you. Stick to that and you will never regret it. You will never be disappointed.

Then, when you are married, you can enjoy the sexual and physical relationship with your spouse. You enjoy it with a clear conscience. You can lay down with your partner in the undefiled marriage bed without being haunted by memories that didn't have to be there.

Here are important things every couple should discuss about the physical aspect of marriage.

1.   Do you know the difference between sex and love?

You can have sex without any love. You can express love without sex. In marriage, sex and love can be a package with the full blessing of God.

2.   Have you read any books on the physical aspects of marriage, or marriage in general?

Some folks think that because they're supposed to stay away from sex before marriage, they should try not to enjoy sex within marriage. That's as unbiblical as adultery. Couples need to be informed about the physical and sexual aspects of marriage. There are a number of books out on how couples can enjoy a sexual relationship at any age. Partners need to talk about those options and discover how to bring each other pleasure as God intended.

3. **What if you discover one partner is more demanding sexually than the other?**

Like everything else in marriage, the physical aspect is a partnership. Couples need to tune in to each other's "passion clock." Sometimes the partner who isn't as excited about sexual activity needs to fulfill the other's desires. Other times, the partner who is more demanding sexually has to wait. But both partners should be looking out for, and accommodating, the other.

4. **Do you both want children? When? How many?**

This is one thing that many couples forget to talk about these days. Going into your marriage, you surely need to agree on if, or how long you will wait before, you have children. You should also have a general idea about how large a family you wish to have, and what that might mean for you in terms of your careers, income and location.

5. **Will you make a commitment from the time you read this question until you are one in Christ, in Christian marriage, to be sexually pure toward one another?**

Treating each other with respect before you are married will carry over into your marriage. Helping each other obey God before you are married will carry over into your marriage. The "right" you *do* now will help you *be* right later.

6. If you have already become intimate, will you confess
    it to the Lord, ask <u>His</u> forgiveness, and for the
    strength to be pure until you are married?

If you're Christians, you need to take the Lord's com-
mands seriously. If you play around with fornication like it
doesn't matter, what <u>will</u> matter? God forgives us when we
ask. That's His promise. And though it may not seem that
staying away from sex really matters once you've been intimate, showing some discipline does.

Now that we've looked at some general ideas about marriage, let's look at some specifics that can be your everyday
recipe to make your marriage all it can be.

MY RECIPE TO GET MARRIED AND STAY MARRIED

You're about to read the "Recipe for a Successful Marriage" I share with couples when they ask for advice about marriage.

Obviously I have experienced what I have written here after being married to one man 56 years. I did not even think about writing principles about marriage until I went through the experience.

A version of this "recipe" of mine ran in *Jet* magazine a few years back. About a month after that article appeared, I got a call at 11:30 a.m. one morning. It was from South Africa. The voice on the other end of the line said, "You don't know me, and I don't know you. Are you Reverend Willie Barrow?"

I said, "Yes."

He said, "I just wanted to call and tell you I subscribe to *Jet* magazine. If I didn't get anything else out of *Jet* magazine this month but your article, I want you to know that you saved my marriage. My wife and I are back together, and based upon your principles we are never separating."

About six months later a girl from Los Angeles called. She said, "Reverend Barrow, I took and read your recipe in *Jet* magazine. I have four children. I have a husband. We are back together. You saved our marriage with this recipe.

"We were having a hard time with money problems. Now we are a loving couple. He has come back to the family, and we both go to church now. You saved my marriage."

If this recipe didn't do anything else but help those two marriages, then developing it was worth it. But I've been told it's helped many other couples over the years. I hope it's worth something to you, too.

One

REMEMBER, MARRIAGE IS A PARTNERSHIP.

When you choose marriage, you should think in terms of choosing a partner first, then a lover. Because suppose your love life ended on a dead-end street through illness or injury? You can still survive as partners in that shipwreck. You can still be partners...

- at home,

- raising your children,

- spoiling your grandchildren,

- in business,

- at church,

- as workers, and

- in companionship.

Marriage is not only just a relationship with a person. It's ideas, it is issues, it's concerns. It's hanging out with someone who has a vision on life where you can be his or her balance. You must think, "Because I am a woman and he is a man, I must see myself as a helpmeet. Just don't take my 'femaleness' for granted. I won't take your 'maleness' for granted. We won't take each other's intellect for granted, either."

Even friendship is a holy connection as God brings two people together for fellowship. How much more is marriage, then? From the get-go, marriage was divine intention; ordered by God all the way from Eve and Adam through your partnership.

Each partner must commit, "Forever I am to be what my spouse needs in a partner." Sometimes partnership is 50/50, 70/30, sometimes it 80/20. It's not always 50/50. It's about giving and balance according to what each partner brings to the marriage that brings about equality.

Partnership is based on function. I love the word "function." It cuts to the heart of what marriage looks like every day. Like I said, I don't think marriage is 50/50. It's according to function. I am an organizer by trade, by profession. The balance I brought to my partner in household organization was sometimes 70/30, sometimes 80/20, sometimes 99/1. I was the organizer at home. When something needed to be organized, I almost always took over that function. Our partnership didn't look equal at all in those moments.

But Clyde was not threatened by that. He understood that I knew organization better than he. But when it came to putting together our estate plans, Clyde took the lead role. He understood those things better than I did. He functioned as our estate planner, and kept up on what was best for us. I'd say again, sometimes his share of partnership in that function was 70% to my 30%, and in some instances more.

Could Clyde have done more organization? Of course. Could I have done more on the estate side? Yes. But I have enough sense, and I know enough about partnerships and associates that I could say we put the estate plans together but he could handle them better. And he knew that I was the organizer in the household.

That's partnership. Knowing your limitations, and knowing what your partner does well can help round out your life.

Questions to Talk Over

1. *What strengths and weaknesses do you (or will you) bring into your marriage? How about your partner?*

2. *With your partner, write down all the things that you are, or will become, partners in as a married couple.*

Notes

_____

_____

_____

_____

_____

_____

_____

Notes

_____

_____

_____

_____

_____

_____

_____

Two

REMEMBER YOUR
VOWS TO LOVE,
CHERISH AND
RESPECT EACH
OTHER.

In most marriage ceremonies, the partners vow to love, cherish and respect each other.

"Just give me my respect," I said to any would-be suitor. You know, I had some pretty strict rules about that. My husband gave me respect before we were married, and continued to do so through our days together. Here were a few habits we developed that helped us remember to respect each other:

- Every day we tried to do something together, even if it was no more than breakfast in the morning (or when my husband was working evenings, dinner together.) That reminded both of us that we needed to show each other the courtesy of listening to each other. Our schedules didn't often mesh, so it was important for us to hold each other in enough esteem to get together and find out how the other partner was doing. What happened during the day? What happened on your job? What happened on your way home? We would discuss basic things like that.

- We never went any place without informing each other. And it wasn't because we were checking up on each other, we were just being respectful of each other. Whatever he wanted to do, he would do it anyway and whatever I wanted to do, I was going to do it anyway! (There's more about this later in the recipe.)

But with respect, there are also vows to love and cherish each other. Sometimes you have to remind yourself just how much your partner means to you. There are even times you have to remind your partner how much you mean to him or her.

How do you stay with one man for 56 years? You just stay there. *I* just stayed there. Because sometimes you must have a forgiving spirit, you have to have an understanding heart, and you just have to be willing to go a little further.

When Jesus was with the disciples and he was tired, he got on his knees to pray. In order to do that, the Bible says Jesus left the disciples and went a little further. Likewise, sometimes you gotta go a little further in your marriage.

Suppose you get frustrated with your present husband, for example. If you go and get another man, the new man might be a drunkard. If you leave that one and go to yet another one, he might be an adulterer. Leave him and go to another one, he might be a drug addict.

When you leave your partner, where are you going? I just stayed there and rectified my situation, starting with my own heart, and then I would let him know.

Once we were really going through some major problems. I knew that something was happening in his life and my life. I knew that he was involved with another lady. I just told him, "Can't no other woman cook like me. Can't no other woman take care of you like me. She ain't good enough. She's not beautiful enough. She don't know enough. I'm the best that you have. You might not realize it right now, but I am your very best."

I kept telling him that over and over, and finally he believed it. Finally he believed it. And that's what kept me there 56 years.

When my husband died he left me an income, the house was paid for, all the bills were paid off, and he left me a legacy of love and respect. Am I glad now I stayed with him? I thank God for our marriage every day.

Don't be running from partner to partner. You know something's wrong with that. Stay with your partner and realize your purpose is to unfold your education, your righteousness, your rightness and, together, run God's world.

Questions to Talk Over

1. *What are some ways you show respect to your partner?*

2. *Do you believe that you love your partner like no one else can? You should. Take a few minutes and write down what you'd tell your partner to prove that point. (Extra credit: When you can, read what you wrote out loud to your partner.)*

Notes

_____

_____

_____

_____

_____

_____

_____

Notes

Three

NEVER PUT
EACH OTHER
DOWN IN
PUBLIC.

There were a lot of things that my husband and I could have pulled out to put each other down.

He could have made fun of my strict moral code. A young woman on her own who wouldn't even let a man touch her? You gotta be kidding. Then she grew up chopping cotton in Texas; just an old country girl who wasn't sophisticated. And she wanted to be a preacher, but she couldn't pay for school! She's a welder! Why isn't she a waitress?

You know something? I never heard a single word like that out of his mouth once we began seeing each other.

I could have brought up that his sisters all had different daddies. I could have made a big deal about him being a foreigner. I could have put him down for never wanting to go out and meet the movers and shakers I was having dinner with because of my job. I could have made fun of how shy he was.

But that isn't how a partnership of love and respect is built.

We didn't put each other down in family experience. You never want to talk about your partner's mama, or express that he's not well-adjusted because of his daddy. You don't want to put down the way he or she dresses.

You can try to put each other down by geography. "Oh, he's from the south." "Oh, she's from the farm." You must be careful with stuff like that. "He's from Haiti." "She's from Jamaica." They are already feeling the pressure of being an immigrant, and then you make it sound like a disease. You reinstate the negatives they feel. Sometimes they don't say anything, but it's in their hearts.

You can't afford to make your partner the butt of your jokes. Period.

You have to be very careful of putting each other down. And especially when the public, even your friends, can draw their own conclusions.

Questions to Talk Over

1. *Are there any sensitive issues that, if you even mentioned them in public, might seem like you are putting down your partner? You need to find out what those are so you can avoid those topics.*

2. *Are there things about yourself that you would rather your partner never talk about in public? You need to let your partner know.*

3. *Does your humor ever seem cruel to your partner? If so, discuss how you can avoid being cruel at other people's expense in the future.*

Notes

_____

_____

_____

_____

_____

_____

_____

Notes

_____

_____

_____

_____

_____

_____

_____

Four

TALK.
WHEN YOU
COMMUNICATE,
THERE IS NO
LIMIT TO WHAT
YOU CAN DO.

Communication is the bottom line of any relationship—on the job, in the church, in your community. Know your neighbor. Know the person who lives upstairs; know the person who lives across the street. Communicate. Talk. When you talk, you can work. When you talk, when you communicate—that is the bottom line.

So, you need to talk in the marriage relationship, too. My husband was considered a slow-talking man. I am like fire, just burn up the words. Then, too, he came from a whole other background. My husband was born in Belize. At that time, it was under the British as British Honduras. Men in many other countries just don't do ordinary housework to be supportive. The women have to do everything. I really helped him make an adjustment, and we had to talk some things over.

But I didn't begin with, "Clyde, we have to talk." A lot of times that's just the wrong thing to do. Instead, you need to create an atmosphere where you can talk. If you lead with, "We gotta talk," too often the first thing your mate thinks is, "You're talking down to me, and *I am not a child*." Then they begin to set up those barriers against talking with you at all.

So you just create the atmosphere. If you know you have to talk, you may get up and fix waffles for your spouse rather than toast. You serve breakfast as an act of love and respect and say, "I thought you might really like this." You create an atmosphere where your mate feels that you are sharing, and not teaching. Mama, Daddy, and Gramma all taught. You're not any one of them. You're his or her partner. You need to share, not teach.

But there are times where, even if you create the atmosphere, it's still difficult to talk about an issue. Then you just need to know how to hush.

A marriage is full of feelings and vision. Sometimes it just takes awhile for your partner to put those into words. You must have enough mental radar to know when your partner isn't ready to talk. Because if they're not ready to talk, asking them to talk just irritates them.

That was a real lesson at first for me, just to hush. When I felt that what I was saying was not being accepted, I had to hush and wait a while. It's hard to be patient. That goes back to the whole concept of married life as a life of hard work and series of adjustments. You still have to learn how to adjust.

When you hear on the inside that the clock has stopped ticking, like the bomb is just about to explode, hush. Otherwise you create a spontaneous combustion; I mean you may fight, start using profanity, start shouting, because you have not learned the science of hushing. It's a science. And I had to learn that. After I learned it, it was just no problem.

Once you've created that atmosphere to talk, you can

bring up the issue. It could be taking out the garbage. It could be, "Honey, please go start up the car so that it can be warm by the time I get out there." If you haven't set the atmosphere to talk, your mate may say, "I don't have to go out there and start up no car. I mean, I am cold just like you. Why do I have to go out there and get cold?"

Then, once you've made your point, don't keep on saying it over and over again. Know when to hush and know when to stop. That keeps down all of this anger and fighting and walking out on each other. It keeps you from dismissing each other as though your partner doesn't matter. Nobody wants to be dismissed.

And it's mostly the little things, not big things, that become issues of communication. It's the little things that must be watched that can destroy you, your marriage, and your entire home. Think about how a child has to deal with your mixed messages, for example. Daddy says you can go out to play; Mama says you can't. So you create the confusion not only between you and your spouse but also between your children and yourself. Then the family is confused and doesn't know who to obey, who to respect, who is saying the truth. They really don't know who is who.

So talk with your partner. Create the right atmosphere for a discussion, and keep talking about everything you can think of. Communication empowers a couple like few other things can.

Questions to Talk Over

1. *Do you think you tend to teach more than share, or share more than teach as you talk to your partner? Ask your partner to verify your answer.*

2. *Talk with your partner about the best ways to create an atmosphere for discussion with each other.*

3. *Are there difficult issues you and your partner need to discuss now? How will you approach that conversation?*

Notes

Notes

_____

_____

_____

_____

_____

_____

_____

Five

DON'T BE
AFRAID TO
COMMEND AND
COMPLIMENT
EACH OTHER.

When was the last time you told your wife how good she looked? When was the last time you told your husband that he's handsome? Every spouse needs to hear that they're attractive to their mate. It's not that hard to say, "Darling, you look so wonderful," or "You are truly my prince." (Or "princess.")

One of the easiest ways to build your marriage is to sincerely commend and compliment each other. It doesn't always have to center around how your spouse looks, either.

Clyde always let me know about how proud he was of my work for social justice. He was the first to say how much he enjoyed it when I was the guest of honor at a banquet, or going somewhere to receive an award in public. Although he was not comfortable himself going everywhere I went, he had a regular circle of friends that he'd call and say, "My wife is out tonight at the Hilton getting an award again!" He made them aware of his pride in me, so they could double up on his compliments to me when I was honored. He was so proud. Eventually, I had a street named after me in Chicago. Clyde wasn't jealous. He told all his friends. He sent pictures back to his family in Belize. Isn't that something?

Although Clyde was very talkative to me, outside the home environment he was not a very talkative person. When he did make up his mind to come with me to an event, I would tell him how proud I was of him. I knew he wasn't comfortable at those events. Wherever I was going, I would always acknowledge my husband. If people acknowledged me I would tell them, "My husband is here tonight." I made sure they gave him the proper attention.

You see, commending your spouse in private is very important. Telling other people how proud you are of your spouse has a power of its own, too. Then you're really putting your mate in a positive light. Your partner sees and hears that you want everyone to know you're married.

Questions to Talk Over

1. *How often do you think you compliment your spouse? Try this: Make a list of all the compliments you give your spouse over the course of a day. Then, evaluate to see if you need to be more complimentary toward your partner.*

2. *What do you tell other people about your spouse? Are your comments mostly positive, or mostly negative? Try to find three good things to say about your partner to someone else today.*

Notes

_____

_____

_____

_____

_____

_____

_____

Notes

_____

_____

_____

_____

_____

_____

_____

Six

TRY NOT TO BE ANGRY AT THE SAME TIME.

Marriage is a series of adjustments. Marriage is hard work. And sometimes, marriage is so frustrating you get angry.

You must have some understanding about the anger you feel, and then you must reach out for some help. I'll never forget an old woman in the church by the name of Mother Lane. I got mad at my husband one day and went to her house. I was going to spend the night with her. It was getting dark, dark, dark.

Finally Mother Lane said, "Willie, it's about time for you to go home."

I said, "Mother Lane, I'm not going home. I came to spend the night. I'm not going to go back to that house to that man."

She said, "You can't stay here. You got cab fare?"

I said, "Yes, ma'am."

And she said, "You go back home."

Today I see that Mother Lane is part of the salvation of my marriage. She wouldn't let me leave. She sent me back where I came from. She said, "You go back. You may not make up tonight, but just you going back after you told him you was leaving will help."

Isn't that something? She was about 80 years old, and she preserved our family by keeping our marriage together. She made me realize that I had the right mind, the right strength. I had what it took to keep my marriage together.

I don't even discuss divorce. "Divorce" means "leave." Well, if you leave, where are you going? Who are you going with? Where are you going to land? What are you leaving? Are you leaving because you got mad? Is that a good reason?

Never go to bed angry. Don't let anger fester up inside you overnight if you can help it. Try not to be angry at the same time, either. Sometimes when both partners get angry at the same time they both leave the house and go their separate ways. Then when one partner's ready to talk it through and make up, the other partner isn't at home.

Somebody's got to give it up, and I was always that some-body. Because number one, I had God. Sometimes I got to bed and I said, "Honey, I'm still mad—and I can't go to sleep being mad."

Somebody's got to be stronger when anger enters the rela-tionship. Try to be that somebody.

Questions to Talk Over

1. How do you handle anger? What can your spouse do to help you get over your anger quickly?

2. How does your spouse handle anger? What can you do to help your spouse get over his/her anger quickly?

3. Can you and your spouse commit to each other now that you will never go to bed angry, but instead at least try to talk your disagreement through? Talk over what practical things you will do to make that commitment a reality.

Notes

_____

_____

_____

_____

_____

_____

_____

Notes

Seven

NEVER USE
SEX AS A
WEAPON.

Never use sex as a weapon. If your husband comes in and you don't like something he's done sometimes women tend to say, "No sex." Sometimes husbands freeze out their wives sexually to make their wives think they're unattractive or failing in the marriage. But that's like you're using sex as a weapon. Sex is not meant for that.

It takes a lot of adjustment to keep a marriage together, and the sexual relationship is one of those adjustments. What is a sexual relationship? It is our relationship as a married couple, as close as we can get physically. Sometimes it's just holding me in your arms. Sometimes it's hearing your spouse whisper in your ear, "Baby, you look so good, you smell so good, I just want to hold you tight."

I can use the sexual relationship as a weapon. Anything that physically puts us at a distance one from the other makes the sexual relationship impossible. I can sleep in another bed. I can announce, "I am going upstairs, downstairs, anywhere not to sleep with you tonight." And you may not even need to say it. You just go upstairs and go to bed. You've announced with your physical distance the distance and loneliness you want your partner to feel. That's a weapon.

Lying down with my mate is a relationship. Lying in the arms of my mate is a relationship. He or she is on the right side or the left side of me, really close; that's a relationship. It's a romantic relationship. It goes beyond the sexual act.

That's why I believe when your spouse isn't able to perform sexually that you don't leave them.

We are all mixed up about relationships. Half the time you don't really know what you need to achieve even when you go through that sexual exercise. You don't get anything out of it, because you don't know what it's for. You need to use sex as a means to build closeness. You need to prefer your partner, not yourself.

As you grow older, you may enjoy physical love with your mate more through holding hands, or a hug. You don't need to try to have a relationship by comparing the old with the new. That time is gone, but your love hasn't gone. There are other things that round out your love over time. That doesn't mean sex goes by the wayside. It just means the romance covers more of your partnership—a real thrill.

Questions to Talk Over

1. *How do you promote physical closeness in your marriage?*

2. *What adjustments did you (or will you) have to make to have a healthy sexual relationship?*

3. *Are there specific things that make you or your partner more likely to say "no sex" as a weapon in your relationship? What can you both do to avoid that response?*

Notes

_____

_____

_____

_____

_____

_____

_____

Notes

_____

_____

_____

_____

_____

_____

_____

Eight

DISAGREE IF YOU MUST, BUT TRY NOT TO BE DISAGREEABLE.

Home is where you live; where you create environment. If you are arguing and fussing and can't get along at home, you take that right to the job, or to church, or to your community club.

When you get married, you have to drop words like "mine," "I," "my car," "my job," even "my life." (We already talked about dropping "my check" earlier.) You need to pick up the words "we" and "ours," especially at home. Why? Because at home we have an agreement: we have come together as one. We don't think altogether alike, but we share a focus. On the weekends, with both of us working, we have to spend time together to come together as one.

My husband and I had a timeshare in Orlando, Florida. He loved to travel. That was one thing we did together. We both loved having people with us at the timeshare. On Sundays, we'd still cook that "Sunday dinner" of beans and rice and plantains. I knew he loved that and we did that together. So we agreed on travel, having people with us and Sunday dinner.

We didn't agree on exercise. I walked five miles and he would walk about a mile. But instead of me fussing at him for not walking the whole way or him fussing at me for walking so much, we agreed to disagree. He would sit and wait on me to finish, and we both did just fine.

We didn't agree about fishing, either. I loved to spend part of our Sundays at the timeshare fishing. For a long time, he didn't. So I went by myself. We disagreed, but weren't being disagreeable about it.

Our time was just too precious to have our differences and disagreements turn into fussing at each other. We found ways to disagree, but not be disagreeable. We let go of arguments we had in the past. If we had something to really talk over, we discussed it—then we let it go.

Questions to Talk Over

1. *How are you and your partner at "agreeing to disagree?"*

2. *What are some of the things you disagree about? What specific things can you do to avoid becoming disagreeable over those things?*

Notes

Notes

_____

_____

_____

_____

_____

_____

_____

Nine

CHECK IN, CALL IN, WITHOUT FEELING THAT YOU'RE CHECKING UP ON EACH OTHER.

Where are you going today? Does your spouse know?

Checking in with your spouse is just common courtesy. It's a simple way to show your partner respect.

As I mentioned earlier, Clyde and I never went any place without informing each other. We weren't checking up on each other. We were just being respectful of each other.

Over the years, Clyde worked different shifts on his job. My work kept me on the road constantly. Even when I was in town, there were many times when I was on my way to a meeting or a banquet where my husband wasn't with me. On many of those occasions, I was formally escorted by other men who had some involvement with the event.

Clyde was never jealous. I never gave him the chance to get jealous. I'd call him every step of the way throughout the evening so he'd know exactly where we were. I'd call him after the evening's event was done to let him know about when I'd be home.

My husband often made it a point to call me during the day just to see how I was doing. It wasn't checking up on me, it was staying in touch. That practice became even more precious to both of us as the years went on.

Those phone calls, day or night, are easier now because so many of us have cell phones. Staying in touch is easier than ever. You don't have to leave your partner in suspense.

Your mate has a right to know where you are.

Questions to Talk Over

1. *What are the best times in the day for phone calls from your partner? Let your spouse know if there are times when you won't be available for the phone (meetings, workout time, etc.).*

2. *When and how often would your partner like to hear from you on a normal workday? When you're on a business trip?*

Notes

_____

_____

_____

_____

_____

_____

_____

Notes

_____

_____

_____

_____

_____

_____

_____

Ten

EDUCATE EACH OTHER ABOUT EACH OTHER'S DESIRES AND NEEDS.

For a marriage to work well, you need to educate each other about each other's desires and needs. You must also realize and own up to each other's limitations or differences.

You are two different people. You're really two different people with two different backgrounds. I had a double whopper in my marriage: not only were we two different people with two different backgrounds, but we also represented two entirely different cultures from different countries. I really had to make some serious adjustments because my husband's background was so different.

I made it my business to go to his country every year to visit his relatives.

The main thing that I studied long before we married was his family. We dated practically five years. During that five years I met him, his mother, his three sisters and his cousin. My husband was not reared with a father. He was reared by his grandmother. He had a whole different outlook on life because he was reared by two women. There was no male model for him. His father was a nice man and everything. He found out about his father after he came to this country. His mother was a schoolteacher. He lived with his grandmom.

All this meant that he was used to women "doing" for him. He had no idea of how a man would treat a woman. He had no background in helping around the house. All those were limitations. I had to calculate, put all this together and find out what approach I had to make in order to mingle his culture into my culture.

I came out of a two-parent home, had grandparents on both sides, came out of a very strict religious atmosphere; very strict. I dated my husband for five years because I was in seminary, and I never kissed him. When I first met him I said, "I don't mind going out with you, but I don't allow any man to put his hands on me." And he took it literally. We were getting off the bus one day and I fell. He never put a hand on me. He just took it literally and let me lay on the ground! So I had to tell him that I didn't mean that if I fell, he wasn't supposed to pick me up.

So maybe one of my limitations was intimidating the man who would be my husband. In our early years of marriage, we had to work through his limitations and my limitations. We had to talk to each other about our desires. I really wanted to set up a budget and buy a house. He let me know that he desired more privacy than I did.

My husband was not an extrovert in any sense of the word. Remember, he was not at all drawn to social events, but I was. Early in our marriage, I compared our marriage to other couples' marriages. I complained about how all the other couples we knew went out together to events. That would irritate him. It almost broke up our marriage, too.

After a while, I realized that I was trying to make him over into someone he would never be. I had to honor his desire to be a more private person, just as he honored my desires to budget and get a house. I learned to accept and appreciate the husband I had. And I never, ever compared us to another married couple again.

Questions to Talk Over

1. Can you name your partner's top three desires and needs? If you can't, talk to your partner and find out what they are.

2. Can your partner name your top three desires and needs? Have you clearly communicated them to your partner? If not, set a time with your partner to discuss them.

3. Are you and your partner aware of each other's limitations? Name them.

Notes

Notes

_____

_____

_____

_____

_____

_____

_____

Eleven

EACH
PARTNER
MUST BE
SEEN AS AN
INDIVIDUAL.

When God creates a marriage partnership, He never intends the partners to lose themselves as individuals.

I believe the individuals making up the partnership need to be seen as they are. There's a time when we were first introduced to others when people may have had to think of us as "Willie's husband" or "Clyde's wife." That was fine at first, and that is true.

But I think you understand by now how important it was for us to help other people see us as individuals. Remember, I took great pride and pleasure in telling people how my husband kept me up on the daily news. (I still brag on him to this day for the wonderful job he did in planning our estate).

And my husband always took the opportunity to tell people about me and what I did. He knew that I was a manager, and not just in my home. I can face any corporation. I can sit with the CEOs and have prayer before any meeting and they have to listen because I know my purpose.

My husband not only let me have a life as an individual, he encouraged me to do so. Because we encouraged each other to be individuals, our partnership was stronger. We each had better ideas about what we really brought into the marriage, and how we fit together as husband and wife.

What do you think of your partner? Do you understand all the strengths he or she has to offer? Do you encourage your partner to step out of your shadow to be recognized as an individual?

Questions to Talk Over

1. *How will you and your partner express your individuality in your marriage?*

2. *What will you do to encourage others to recognize your partner as an individual?*

Notes

_____

_____

_____

_____

_____

_____

_____

Notes

_____

_____

_____

_____

_____

_____

Twelve

DON'T TRY TO MAKE YOUR MATE OVER. (IT CAN'T BE DONE.)

Sometimes I hear people talk about an "ideal mate." After 56 years of marriage, I still don't know what that means.

Nobody's perfect. Everybody makes mistakes. Everyone has flaws.

My husband could have been more outgoing. I wanted to change that about him early in our marriage. But trying to change that didn't just irritate him; it almost broke up our marriage.

There are times, plenty of times, I wish my husband would have walked just a piece farther with me when we had the chance. I wish he would have gone fishing with me more often, and started that earlier in our marriage. But how do you make someone like something they don't care to do? And if you could, is it right to force your way on them?

If I could have changed anything about my husband, it was that he smoked and drank. Those habits together were the biggest problem I ever had with my husband. Eventually he stopped. He really stopped, though he didn't think he could really stop. He stopped after his habits had already affected his lungs. He died of lung cancer.

But then I have to think about how my husband never really tried to make me over, either. He let me travel the world while he stayed home. He stayed informed about my work, even the details. He let me have a lot of spotlight and never got jealous.

He had a real appreciation for me; not even for himself, but for me. And I stuck around for 56 years with Clyde Raymond Barrow. I think I appreciated him more and more every day until 1997. That's when I lost him.

I would not be the woman I am today without him. It was God who made him unusual. It was God who made him special for me. So I thank God for him.

And you thank God for your partner, too.

Questions to Talk Over

1. *Assuming that your partner won't try to make you over, what changes are you willing to make that will please him or her?*

2. *What about your partner may not be attractive to everyone else, but is just right for you?*

Notes

_____

_____

_____

_____

_____

_____

_____

Notes